CONTINENTS

ANTARCTICA

John Baines

RSVP

**RAINTREE
STECK-VAUGHN**
P U B L I S H E R S
The Steck-Vaughn Company

Austin, Texas

CONTINENTS

AFRICA   EUROPE

ANTARCTICA   NORTH AMERICA

ASIA   SOUTH AMERICA

AUSTRALIA & OCEANIA

Published by Raintree Steck-Vaughn Publishers, an imprint of Steck-Vaughn Company

Library of Congress Cataloging-in-Publication Data
Baines, John D.
Antarctica / John Baines.
    p.   cm.—(Continents)
    Includes bibliographical references and index.
    Summary: Examines the geography, wildlife, resources, conservation, and potential development of the roughly circular continent that surrounds the South Pole.
    ISBN 0-8172-4782-3
    1. Antarctica—Juvenile literature.
    [1. Antarctica.]
    I. Title. II. Series (Austin, Tex.)
    G863.B35 1997
    919.8'9—dc21   96-52704

Printed in Italy. Bound in the United States.
1 2 3 4 5 6 7 8 9 0 02 01 00 99 98

ACKNOWLEDGMENTS
The author would like to thank the British Antarctic Survey and Greenpeace for the information they supplied to help in the writing of this book.

Picture Acknowledgments
Bryan and Cherry Alexander 6, 7, 17, 29 (Ann Hawthorne), 32 (David Rootes), 36 (Ann Hawthorne), 37(NASA), 38, 41; ET Archive 22; Hedgehog House, NZ 5 (Sabine Schmidt), 11 (Colin Monteath), 13 (Colin Monteath), 16 (Stefan Lundgren), 30 (Mark Mabin), 33 (Kim Westerskov), 35 (Paul Ensor), 39 (Colin Monteath), 40 top (Colin Monteath), 40 bottom (Kerry Lorimer), 44 (Kim Westerskov); Mary Evans Picture Library 23, 24; Oxford Scientific Films 9 (Bruce Herrod), 14 (Tui de Roy), 19 (Kim Westerskov), 27 bottom (Rick Price), 34 (Ben Osborne), 43 (Ben Osborne); Popperfoto 25, 27 top; Still Pictures 18 (Vincent Bretagnolle), 31 (Bryan and Cherry Alexander), 42 (David Hoffman), 45 (Roland Seitre); Tony Stone Images 4 (John Beatty), 10 (Ben Osborne), 21 (Art Wolfe); Zefa 15 (Hummel), 20.

Artwork by Peter Bull
Graph artwork by Mark Whitchurch

CONTENTS

INTRODUCTION

The dramatic landscape of the Antarctic Peninsula. Summer temperatures here can reach up to 59° F.

Most people know that it is very cold in Antarctica. What is less well known is how the cold makes this continent so different from the others. One look at the table of facts and figures is enough to tell us that Antarctica is unlike anywhere else. It is a place where people have made very little change to the environment, and this raises questions about how to deal with Antarctica in the future. Should it remain a protected area, like a national park, and be used only for peaceful scientific research, or should it be developed as most other parts of the earth have been?

Temperatures in Antarctica are far lower than those inside a home freezer. In such cold conditions, strange things can happen to familiar materials. For example, if a solid steel bar is dropped it can shatter like a piece of glass.

A UNIQUE PLACE

Thickness of ice at the South Pole	9,100 ft.
Average annual temperature inland	−70° F
Lowest recorded temperature (world record)	−128.5° F
Area with monthly average temperature above 32° F	0 acres
Area used for farming	0 acres
Area covered by forest	0 acres
Area covered by lakes	0 acres
People living permanently in Antarctica	0
Year first visited by humans	1821

STRANGE SIGHTS IN ANTARCTICA

The cold of Antarctica can cause some spectacular optical illusions. The air holds millions of tiny ice crystals, and these can create phenomena such as mock suns, in which the sun appears to be surrounded by a huge wheel of light and an "extra" sun on either side.

Rays of light can sometimes bounce between the ice and low clouds, creating a "white-out," in which it is impossible to see anything. Mirages, which are normally seen in hot deserts, can also appear in Antarctica.

Left *Parhelions, or mock suns, at Erebus Bay on Ross Island. Optical illusions like this occur when light is reflected by ice crystals in the earth's atmosphere.*

As well as being the coldest continent, Antarctica is also one of the driest and windiest. Strong winds are common, and speeds of more than 185 mph have been recorded. For the first Antarctic expeditions, the wind was often a greater problem than the cold. Most explorers have referred to the crippling exasperation of battling against the constant gale-force winds, which make it difficult to walk in a straight line or even to stand up. Winds also blow loose snow into the air and make it impossible to see far. Cold winds also chill the body, and every 1.2 mph increase in the wind speed is equivalent to a 1.8° F drop in temperature.

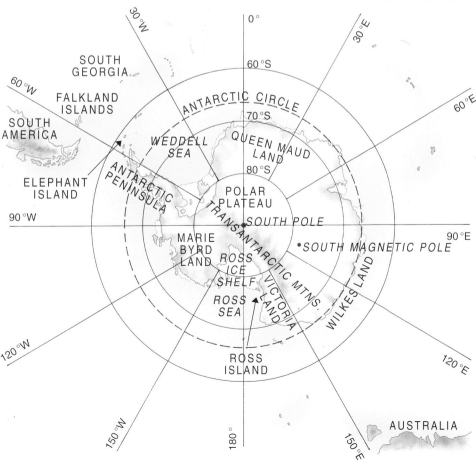

Right *The Arctic and Antarctic regions. The Arctic Circle is an imaginary line drawn at latitude 66° 32' North, and the Antarctic Circle is at 66° 32' South. Because the Arctic and Antarctic are at opposite poles of the earth, when it is winter in one region it is summer in the other.*

NORTH POLE

RUSSIA

GREENLAND

EUROPE

0   1,000 km
0   600 miles

ANTARCTICA

+ SOUTH POLE

0   1,000 km
0   600 miles

ANTARCTIC CIRCLE

Below *Emperor penguins and their chicks sitting on the ice under the midnight sun in Atka Bay, Weddell Sea. There is little food for animals on the land, so they live on fish from the sea.*

THE ARCTIC AND THE ANTARCTIC

The two polar regions have some similarities: They are both cold and covered in ice, and they both have long days during the summer months and long nights in the winter months. However, there are many more differences between them than similarities. The Arctic ice floats on the water of the Arctic Ocean, whereas under the Antarctic ice there is land. In the Arctic region there are native peoples; Antarctica has no permanent inhabitants. Minerals, such as oil, are mined in the Arctic, but there is no mining in Antarctica, even though resources such as coal are known to exist. In the Arctic there is a wealth of wildlife both on the land and in the sea. In the Antarctic, there is so little ice-free land that there are very few species of plants and animals, although the surrounding seas are very rich in wildlife.

THE SIZE OF THE CONTINENTS (sq. mi.)

Asia	17,351,146
Africa	11,711,329
North America	9,074,060
South America	6,880,492
Antarctica	5,483,049
Europe	4,064,020
Australia	2,966,365

POSITION, SHAPE, AND SIZE

Antarctica is the fifth largest of the continents. In summer it covers an area of about 5.48 million square miles, almost half as big again as Europe. In winter it appears to double in size as ice sheets spread out across the surrounding sea. The continent is roughly circular and surrounds the South Pole. The Antarctic Peninsula—the only substantial piece of land lying outside the Antarctic Circle—juts out toward the tip of South America. The Ross Sea and the Weddell Sea form two large indentations in the coastline.

The name Antarctica is normally used to describe the continent and the sea around it. The boundary of the ocean surrounding Antarctica is where its cold waters meet the warmer waters of the Atlantic, Pacific, and Indian oceans.

Above *Pack ice in the midnight sun. During the height of summer there is daylight for 24 hours.*

DAYS AND NIGHTS, WINTER AND SUMMER

The earth spins in space. Once every 24 hours it spins around its axis—an imaginary line between the North and South poles. The earth's axis is tilted over at an angle, so when the Northern Hemisphere is tilted toward the sun, the Southern Hemisphere is tilted away, and vice versa. The earth also orbits the sun, taking one year to make each complete orbit.

During December, when the Northern Hemisphere is tilted away from the sun, the Southern Hemisphere is tilted toward the sun. More than half the Southern Hemisphere is in daylight.

During one 24-hour rotation of the earth, any place in the Southern Hemisphere will stay longer in daylight than in darkness. Inside the Antarctic Circle in December (the middle of summer in the Southern Hemisphere) the sun does not set, and at the South Pole there are six months of continuous daylight.

By June, the earth has moved around to the opposite side of the sun, and the Northern Hemisphere is facing the sun. At the South Pole there are six months of continuous darkness during which the sun never rises above the horizon.

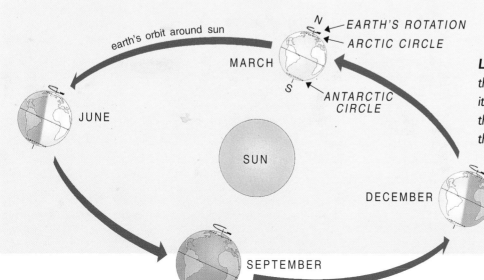

earth's orbit around sun

MARCH

N ← EARTH'S ROTATION
— ARCTIC CIRCLE

S ↙ ANTARCTIC CIRCLE

JUNE

SUN

DECEMBER

SEPTEMBER

Left *The earth moves around the sun, spinning on its axis as it goes. It is tilted in relation to the sun, and this accounts for the way in which the lengths of the days and nights change throughout the year.*

THE GEOGRAPHY OF ANTARCTICA

In recent years, geologists have found that there are deposits of coal in the Transantarctic Mountains. Most coal was made about 300 million years ago, in places where the climate was warm and wet and where there were a lot of plants. When the plants died, they decomposed slowly under water. Layer upon layer built up, and these were then crushed under the weight of other deposits that were being laid on top. Today in Antarctica there are very few plants, and most of the surface is covered by ice—not the conditions in which coal forms. So how did the coal get there?

CONTINENTAL DRIFT

Three hundred million years ago, the earth looked very different from the way it does today. The land consisted of several large continents, including Gondwanaland, Laurasia, and Angaraland, with smaller fragments of continents between them. What is now Antarctica was then a part of Gondwanaland, and it did not lie at the earth's South Pole. It was at this time, when Antarctica was covered with dense vegetation, that the coal deposits began to develop. Since then, the continents have moved about and split apart, thanks to a process known as continental drift. A few million years ago, Antarctica moved to the southernmost part of the globe, and its huge ice sheets began to form. All the continents are still moving, and in another 100 million years Antarctica may have moved closer to the equator and could have a tropical climate.

The world 200 million years ago

LAURASIA

GONDWANALAND

ANTARCTICA

The world 135 million years ago

LAURASIA

N. America
Europe
Siberia
China

S. America
Africa
India

GONDWANALAND

Australia

ANTARCTICA

The world today

ANTARCTICA

Left *The positions of the earth's continents—including Antarctica—have shifted dramatically during the last 200 million years.*

THE HIDDEN LANDSCAPE

It is difficult to study the geology of Antarctica because around 98 percent of it is covered by ice. Much of the information about the ground beneath the ice has come from seismic research. This involves setting off small explosions at the surface and measuring the sound waves that travel down through the ice and rebound from the rocks below back up to the surface. Scientists can use the measurements to work out what the landscape and rocks are like below the ice. Today, scientists can study the landscape under the ice from airplanes, using radio waves instead of sound waves.

THE LAND BENEATH THE ICE

Antarctica is the highest of the world's continents, with an average height above sea level of about 7,500 ft. However, if all the ice were to be removed, it would probably only be about 1,600 ft. above sea level.

If the ice were to be removed from Antarctica, two main areas would be revealed. The largest area, in the Eastern Hemisphere, consists of a platform of very old rocks on top of which younger rocks have been deposited. It would be a huge lowland plain with a central range of mountains called the Gamburtsev Mountains, which are completely covered by ice, and another range of mountains on the coast. The smaller area, in the Western Hemisphere, is really five separate blocks joined by ice. The remaining land, the Antarctic Peninsula, is really an extension of the South American continent. It is a remnant of a volcanic area that was active until 10 million years ago.

Above Scientists carrying out experiments to calculate the thickness of the ice

THE LAND ABOVE THE ICE

Between eastern and western Antarctica, the Transantarctic Mountains run for more than 2,175 mi. across the continent from the Ross Sea to the Weddell Sea. The mountain chain varies in width from 60 to 185 mi. and is made up of several ranges of mountains, although only the highest peaks can be seen above the ice. The bare rock makes a stark contrast with the bright, shiny ice. The highest peak is Vinson Massif at 16,000 ft. Some of the mountain valleys are filled with huge glaciers that carry ice toward the sea.

Right A drawing that shows the main features of the landscape

POLAR PLATEAU

MT. EREBUS

McMURDO SOUND

TRANSANTARCTIC MTNS.

ROSS ICE SHELF

ANTARCTIC PENINSULA — VINSON MASSIF

ROSS SEA

The small areas of land in Antarctica that are ice free are found around the coast and on the steep slopes of the mountains. Around McMurdo Sound, for example, there are river valleys that are dry for most of the year—and even some lakes, although the water in them is very salty. Even in these ice-free areas, the influence of the extreme weather conditions can be seen. On sunny days, the rock can become warm enough to melt the surrounding snow and ice. The meltwater runs down the rocks and seeps into cracks where, out of the sun, it freezes again quickly. As the water freezes it expands, and the force of the expansion can break off chunks of rock that pile up at the bottom of slopes. The only large area of ice-free land is on the Antarctic Peninsula.

Below A boat at dawn off the Antarctic Peninsula, the most accessible part of Antarctica

Above A climber on Brunhilde Peak looks out to the Olympus Range in Victoria Land, Antarctica.

FIRE AND ICE

There are at least two active volcanoes with peaks rising above the ice. The highest, Mount Erebus, at 12,500 ft., is situated near McMurdo Sound. It was discovered in 1841 by James Clark Ross (who named the Ross Sea). He wrote in his diary: "January 27, 1841. Discovered a mountain more than 12,400 feet above sea level, emitting flames and smoke in great profusion, a most grand spectacle."

CLIMATE AND WEATHER

Antarctica is the world's coldest continent: Temperatures there are 50° to 85° F colder than at similar latitudes in the Northern Hemisphere. The warmest part of the continent is the Antarctic Peninsula, where during a "hot" summer the temperature can rise to 59° F. Antarctica is also the windiest continent. At Cape Denison, for example, the average wind speed is 42 mph, compared with 10.5 mph in a typical European town. Ernest Shackleton nearly became the first person to reach the South Pole in 1909, but the winds and the cold proved too much. In his diary for January 9, 1909 (mid-summer in Antarctica) he wrote: "A blinding, shrieking blizzard all day, with the temperature ranging from –60° F to –70° F of frost."

The ice helps keeps the region cold because it does not absorb much heat from the sun. Even when the air is well below freezing point, people standing in the sun can feel very warm because their clothes absorb the sun's heat.

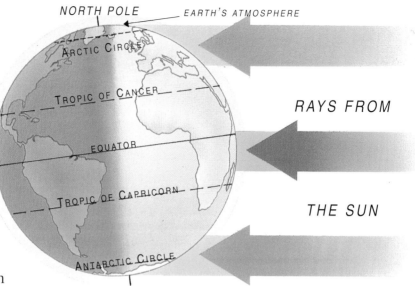

Above *Temperatures at the poles are always lower than at the equator. This is partly because the sun's rays are more spread out at the poles, and they also have a longer route through the earth's atmosphere, which absorbs much of their heat.*

ANTARCTICA AND THE WORLD'S CLIMATE

Antarctica plays a very important part in regulating the climate over the earth as a whole. Winds and ocean currents transfer heat around the globe and help regulate temperatures. Without these movements, the tropical regions would be hotter and the polar regions colder.

Right *The circulation of the air in the Southern Hemisphere. The movements help transfer heat from the hottest parts of the earth's surface toward cooler areas.*

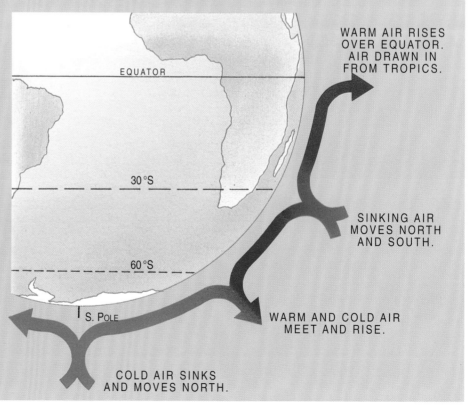

WARM AIR RISES OVER EQUATOR. AIR DRAWN IN FROM TROPICS.

SINKING AIR MOVES NORTH AND SOUTH.

WARM AND COLD AIR MEET AND RISE.

COLD AIR SINKS AND MOVES NORTH.

THE ANTARCTIC DESERT

The interior of Antarctica is one of the driest deserts in the world, with less than the equivalent of 2 inches of rain a year. The air is too cold to hold much moisture. Even at the coast, where temperatures in summer are higher, precipitation is only the equivalent of about 15 inches of rain a year. Only in the Antarctic Peninsula is rain as common as snow.

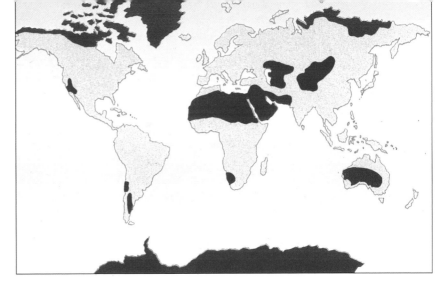

Above The shaded areas on this map all receive fewer than 10 inches of precipitation a year.

COLD COMFORT?

Life in the Antarctic is very difficult because of the cold. The cold makes people weaker and less energetic, and wearing bulky clothing makes doing anything difficult. Doctors suggest that –40° F is the lowest temperature at which people can work effectively outside. However, humans are very adaptable to changes in temperature. We can generate more body heat by exercising, and our bodies even have an in-built form of exercise—shivering—that happens automatically when we get cold. Plenty of food is also essential for survival in the cold: A person working in Antarctica needs to consume about 5,000 calories a day compared with 3,500 in a temperate climate.

People also need special clothing to protect themselves from the cold. When flesh gets very cold, it freezes and no blood can reach it. If left, the flesh begins to rot. Many explorers of the polar regions have lost fingers or toes from frostbite. Another problem is snow blindness—a very painful, temporary blindness caused by the reflection of ultraviolet light from the ice. Explorers and scientists working outside must wear dark goggles to protect their eyes.

Below Warm clothing is essential in Antarctica. At -40° F it does not take long for the cold to freeze bare skin and for icicles to form on eyebrows and beards. Even during the summer a person's breath freezes instantly.

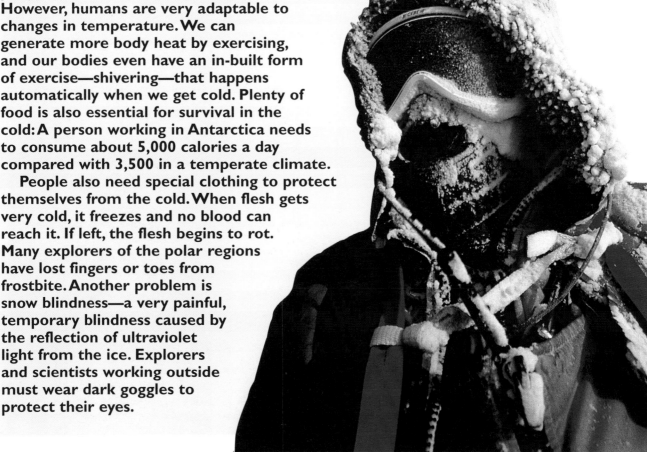

ICE FROM THE LAND

Most of the snow that falls on Antarctica does not melt; it settles and accumulates in layers. The weight of each new layer of snow helps to crush the snow underneath and turns it to ice. Over millions of years, the ice has built up to an average depth of about 1.2 mi. The quantity of ice this represents is staggering. It is 90 percent of all the ice in the world, and 70 percent of all the fresh water. If the Antarctic ice were to melt, the sea level would rise by 215 ft.

The ice would be even thicker were it not for the ability of ice to flow downhill, rather like water. However, it usually only moves a few feet a year, but a glacier can move up to 3 miles a year. The ice moves toward the sea. But it does not stop there, as the weight of the ice behind keeps pushing it forward, out to sea. It grinds along the sea floor until it reaches water deep enough for it to float.

This is the tongue, or tip, of a glacier at the point where it meets the sea. Antarctica has many such glaciers.

The ice flowing out from the land has created huge ice shelves. The one stretching over the Ross Sea covers an area about the same size as France or Texas. At the seaward end, where the ice shelves meet warmer waters, huge pieces of ice break off, forming icebergs that are blown out to sea by the offshore winds.

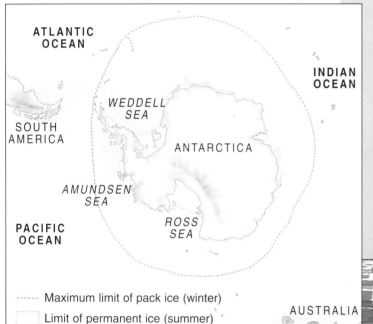

ATLANTIC
OCEAN

INDIAN
OCEAN

WEDDELL
SEA

SOUTH
AMERICA

ANTARCTICA

AMUNDSEN
SEA

PACIFIC
OCEAN

ROSS
SEA

AUSTRALIA

----- Maximum limit of pack ice (winter)

☐ Limit of permanent ice (summer)

Above The area covered by the Antarctic ice increases in the winter months because large areas of the sea become frozen.

FREEZING SEA

The ice on the oceans around Antarctica does not only come from the land. In places, the seawater is so cold that its surface freezes to a depth of several feet. Some sea areas are frozen all year round. In the winter, blocks of floating ice start to form around the edges of the frozen sea. As the temperature falls further, the blocks increase in size and join together to form pack ice. Ships can find themselves trapped by the ice because the frozen surface can spread at more than 2.5 mi. a day.

Right Icebergs are a dramatic feature of Antarctica, and they are usually much larger than icebergs in the Arctic.

OCEANS

The influence of the extremely low temperatures of Antarctica extends to the ocean surrounding the continent. Although there is no physical boundary to see in the water, there are marked differences between the waters around Antarctica and the Indian, Atlantic, and Pacific oceans.

Antarctic winds drive the cold surface waters north, and they meet the south-flowing subtropical waters. The boundary where they meet is known as the Antarctic Convergence, and it lies about 1,200 mi. off the Antarctic shore. The speed at which the Antarctic winds meet the warmer air from the north sets off huge storms over the oceans. Sailors traveling around Cape Horn, at the tip of South America, have learned to fear these storms.

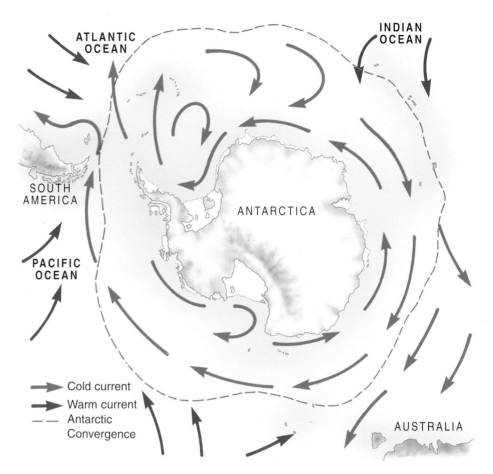

Cold current
Warm current
- - - Antarctic Convergence

Above *Warm and cold surface currents meet at the Antarctic Convergence.*

Below *The sea around Antarctica has the largest waves, the strongest winds, and the most powerful currents on Earth.*

Even the most modern icebreakers can only reach the Antarctic continent during the summer months. The winter is too hazardous, with seas freezing to solid pack ice in just a few hours.

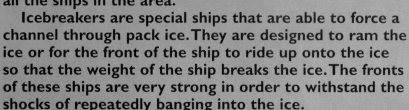

ICE AND SHIPS

Icebergs—blocks of floating ice that have broken off from the main ice sheet or a glacier— are common in the waters around Antarctica. They come in all shapes and sizes and can tower up to 500 ft. above the water. Even so, 90 percent of an iceberg is below the surface. Icebergs are hazards to ships because they move with the ocean currents and cannot be marked on navigation charts. As most of the iceberg is under water, its shape cannot be seen. Radar is used to help locate icebergs, and information about their positions is passed on to all the ships in the area.

Icebreakers are special ships that are able to force a channel through pack ice. They are designed to ram the ice or for the front of the ship to ride up onto the ice so that the weight of the ship breaks the ice. The fronts of these ships are very strong in order to withstand the shocks of repeatedly banging into the ice.

Where the two ocean currents meet, there is a noticeable change in the temperature of the water of between 3.5° and 7° F. When they meet, the warmer water turns east, driven by the westerly winds. The cold water sinks below the warm water, and some of it carries on moving north at the bottom of the ocean. Antarctic waters have been detected on the ocean bed as far north as Bermuda in the Northern Hemisphere. The Antarctic water is less salty than the warmer subtropical waters to the north. This is because there is less evaporation of the seawater in the lower temperatures of the Antarctic and also because ice does not dissolve minerals out of the rocks it passes over on its way to the sea.

WILDLIFE IN ANTARCTICA

Antarctica supports fewer plants and animals than similar harsh areas in the Arctic. This is because Antarctica is much more isolated than the Arctic from other land areas. Plants and animals from Africa, South America, and Australia have not been able to cross the ocean barrier to colonize it.

Above *There is very little plant life in Antarctica, because conditions are too cold and dry and there is almost no soil. Low-growing plants, lichens, mosses, and fungi appear as the ice melts in the summer.*

THE ANTI-FREEZE MITE

The largest land animal in Antarctica is about 1 mm long—just about large enough to be seen without a microscope. It is a mite, and it is able to survive the freezing temperatures by producing chemicals that prevent its blood from freezing. However, there are very few of these tiny creatures because there is not much food available.

LIFE ON LAND

Plants and lichens are the base of every food chain. Without them, no animals would exist. In Antarctica there are only two types of flowering plants—a grass and a plant called *Colobanthus*—and the remainder of the 350 or so plant species are lichens and mosses. They all manage to survive in those few areas where the land or rocks are free of ice and snow in summer. Because there are so few plants, Antarctica cannot support many land animals.

LIFE IN AND ABOVE THE SEA

Although it is very cold, the ocean surrounding Antarctica is rich in the nutrients needed for plants to grow and is able to support a wealth of wildlife. Tiny plants called phytoplankton grow in the surface waters during summer. They are eaten by tiny creatures such as krill, a shrimplike animal that grows to a length of about 2.3 in. The Antarctic krill is probably the most important animal in the ocean because of its vital role in the food chain. Krill form huge swarms that may contain millions of tons of food for larger predators such as seals, seabirds, fish, and whales.

MAMMALS

Whales, dolphins, porpoises, and seals are the only mammals that live naturally in Antarctica. Layers of fat called blubber insulate their bodies from the cold. Their shape has adapted to the marine environment as well: Their arms and legs have shrunk and become fins or flippers, and their bodies have become beautifully streamlined.

Seals get all their food from the sea, but they breed, molt, and rest out of the water, on the ice or on the land. Most of their food consists of krill and fish, but some seals, such as leopard seals, eat penguins and other seals as well. Six species of seals live in Antarctica, and all are now common. During the 19th century, Antarctic fur seals were hunted almost to extinction for their fur, but now that they are protected their numbers have risen to about 1.5 million. Seals are great divers. Elephant seals with electronic recorders attached to them have been recorded at depths of 5,000 ft. below the surface and have stayed under the water without coming up to breathe for two hours.

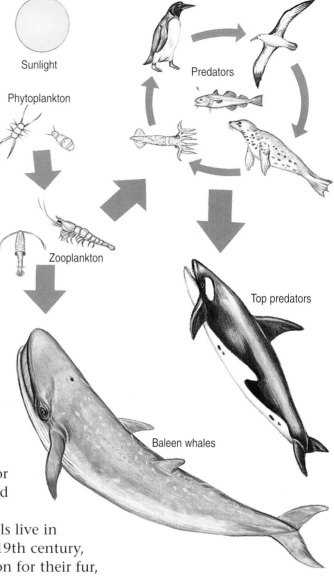

Sunlight

Phytoplankton

Zooplankton

Predators

Top predators

Baleen whales

Above The food web of the ocean surrounding Antarctica. Tiny phytoplankton, such as algae, take the energy they need to grow from sunlight. Krill and other zooplankton eat the phytoplankton and are eaten by larger predators such as penguins, fish, and seals (some of which also eat each other) and by baleen whales. The penguins and seals are, in turn, eaten by killer whales and leopard seals.

Left A Weddell seal eating an Antarctic cod. These seals may dive up to 2,500 ft. to catch fish, octopus, and squid.

Above *A humpback whale and its calf. Antarctic humpbacks migrate to warmer seas in the winter and return to the coastal waters in the summer to feed on krill.*

WHALES

Whales spend all their lives in the sea. Even their young are born under the water and have to be brought to the surface to take their first breaths of air. There are dozens of species of whales. The largest is the blue whale, which grows up to 100 ft. in length and can weigh 150 tons. It is the largest animal ever to live on Earth.

There are two types of whale—baleen whales and toothed whales. Baleen whales have no teeth. Their mouths contain plates of baleen, or whalebone, which act like a sieve, collecting tiny sea creatures from the huge amounts of seawater that pass through. Traveling through the water, a whale can reach speeds of 50 mph. A human scuba diver has to work hard to reach 6 mph. Sperm whales dive to more than 3,200 ft. and can stay submerged for 90 minutes at a time. A human being finds it hard to hold one breath for more than a minute.

WHALES OF THE SOUTHERN OCEANS

Species	Length (feet)	Food	Numbers left
BALEEN WHALES			
blue whale	100 ft.	krill	10–12,000
southern right whale	42–55 ft.	small plankton	few thousand
fin whale	69–72 ft.	krill	85–100,000
sei whale	49–59 ft.	mixed	rare
minke	26 ft.	krill	400,000
humpback whale	39–46 ft.	krill	5,000
TOOTHED WHALES			
sperm whale	36–65 ft.	squid, fish	1,000,000
Amoux's beaked whale	up to 32 ft.	not known	not known
southern bottlenose whale	up to 23 ft.	squid	abundant
killer whale/orca	20–26 ft.	fish to large whales	several thousand
long-finned pilot whale	13–20 ft.	mainly squid	several 100,000

Right *Some of the whales that live in the oceans around Antarctica*

humpback whale ▶

sei whale ▼

Bryde's whale ▼

fin whale ◀

blue whale ▼

minke whale ▼

BIRDS

All the birds of Antarctica depend on the sea for their food. They are able to dive and swim under the water to catch fish, squid, and other creatures. Many of the birds migrate to and from the Antarctic because in winter there is less food there for them and temperatures are lower. The Arctic tern manages to have summer all year by migrating back and forth between the polar regions, completing about 18,500 mi. a year.

The best-known birds in the Antarctic are penguins. Unable to fly, they spend all year in Antarctica and have adapted to survive and breed in the harsh conditions. Their bodies have plenty of fat to protect them from the cold. Their wings have become flat, stiff flippers that are able to propel their streamlined bodies through the water after a fish or a squid. While in the water, their legs and tails act as rudders. Their walking on land is more of a waddle, and they find it easier to slide down the ice into the water on their bellies. There are 16 different species of penguin, varying in size from 16 in. to 45 in. tall. The two largest—king and emperor penguins —can swim to depths of 1,000 ft.

Incubating eggs is not easy in such a cold climate, but the penguins have developed very successful techniques. For example, the female emperor penguin lays a single egg at the start of the winter. The egg is then taken over by the male, who puts it on his feet. A large fold of skin hangs down over it to keep it warm. Thousands of males often huddle together with their eggs to keep one another warm. Once the chick is hatched, the parents take turns keeping it warm and getting food for it from the sea.

When a female Emperor penguin returns from the sea, she and her newly hatched chick must recognize each other's call. She bends her head low to call to the chick, which responds with ear-piercing whistles.

DISCOVERY AND EXPLORATION

WHO WENT WHERE?

Many parts of Antarctica were named after the explorers who first discovered them, including the Ross Sea after the British explorer James Clark Ross, Wilkes Land after the American Charles Wilkes, and the Amundsen Sea after the Norwegian Roald Amundsen. Sometimes places were named after the monarch of a country, such as Victoria Land after the British queen and Queen Maud Land after the queen of Norway.

Antarctica is the coldest continent and the most isolated from other populated areas. It is ringed by the world's stormiest seas and for much of the year is cut off by impenetrable masses of pack ice. It is no wonder that for centuries people could only guess that there might be a continent there and called it *Terra Australis Incognita,* or unknown southern land.

Whalers in Antarctica in the 19th century stripping the blubber off a whale. For those in the small catcher boats, hunting whales was dangerous work.

A CONTINENT CONFIRMED

Whale hunters and seal hunters were the first to discover Antarctica. The first known landing was in 1821 by an American seal hunter. Two years later, a whaling ship captained by James Weddell discovered the sea that now carries his name. By the 1830s all the reports from whale and seal hunters seemed to suggest there was a continent surrounding the South Pole, and several countries sent official expeditions. All the early expeditions took place during the less harsh summer months. In 1899 members of the British Southern Cross Expedition became the first people to spend the winter ashore on Antarctica.

In the early years of the 20th century, there was great interest in scientific investigation of Antarctica, especially the earth's South Magnetic Pole. Great Britain, Sweden, and Germany all sent research groups to Antarctica. Great Britain's first expedition, in 1904–7, was led by Commander Robert Falcon Scott, who later died while attempting to be the first to reach the South Pole.

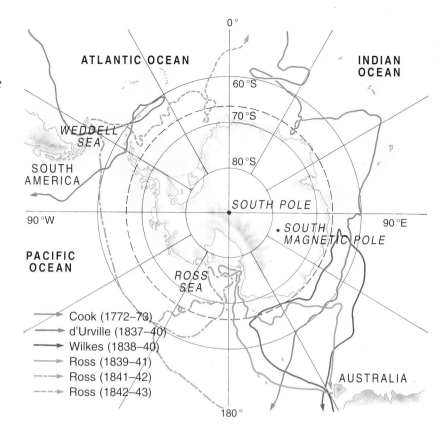

Above *Routes of the earliest Antarctic explorers*

Cook (1772–73)
d'Urville (1837–40)
Wilkes (1838–40)
Ross (1839–41)
Ross (1841–42)
Ross (1842–43)

SHACKLETON

Ernest Shackleton was the first person to organize an expedition to the South Pole. His party set out from McMurdo Sound in October 1908. Shackleton planned to use Siberian ponies to pull the sleds, but by the time he started most of them had died and the remainder only survived for six weeks. To make the round-trip of about 1,675 mi., the explorers would have to haul the sleds most of the way themselves. They made a tremendous effort and by January 9, 1909 were within 100 mi. of the pole. They had little strength left after hauling the sleds, enduring low temperatures and high altitudes, and having little food to eat. Reluctantly, they decided to turn around and try to get back. They lost their way in blizzards and were suffering from frostbite, snow blindness, and dysentery, but they just made it back to safety.

Left *Ernest Shackleton and his men had to haul their sleds up the rim of the polar plateau on their route toward the South Pole.*

THE RACE TO THE POLE

Following Ernest Shackleton's 1908–9 expedition (see page 23), the next attempts on the South Pole were made simultaneously by two separate groups. Roald Amundsen led a Norwegian expedition, and Robert Falcon Scott commanded a British expedition.

Amundsen's triumph

On October 19, 1911, Amundsen's group set off from its base in the Bay of Whales, on the opposite side of the Ross Ice Shelf from Scott's camp at McMurdo Sound. Amundsen set up plenty of supply dumps on the way to the pole, to ensure that there would not be any shortages on the return journey. He decided that the Eskimo practice of using dogs to pull sleds in the Arctic would also work well in Antarctica and started out with four sleds and 52 dogs. Their trip went very smoothly. For the first 100 mi. or so the men rode on the sleds. For the next 300 mi. they were pulled along on skis, letting the dogs do all the hard work. They climbed up onto the Antarctic plateau and there killed all but 18 of the dogs and made a meat store for the return journey. On December 14 the party reached the South Pole and left a tent and a note for Scott, should he turn up later. Their return journey was largely uneventful.

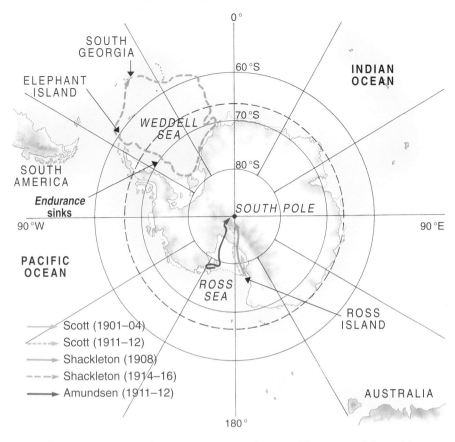

Above The routes followed by Shackleton, Scott, and Amundsen in their attempts to reach the South Pole and the route of Shackleton's failed Imperial Trans-Antarctic Expedition

Below Roald Amundsen and his men raise the Norwegian flag at the South Pole in 1911.

Scott's disaster

Meanwhile, Scott's attempt on the pole was not going well. He did not share Amundsen's faith in dogs and was relying on human strength to pull the sleds, which weighed 350 lbs.—the weight of two adults—for most of the 1,675-mi. journey. The ponies that he planned to use for the start of the journey and setting up supply depots got stuck in the snow and had to be shot. Another problem was the weather, which was so dreadful that the expedition was forced to shelter in tents, losing time and using a lot of precious resources.

On June 6, 1911 Captain Scott celebrated his birthday with his men during their ill-fated expedition to the South Pole.

They struggled on, and about 155 mi. from the pole the last support team started its journey back to base. As Scott and his men drew near the pole, the effects of the weather and the effort of hauling the sleds were causing their strength to decline. It sometimes took them nine hours to strike and pitch camp. Extracts from Scott's diary show how hard they were finding it: "The rest of the afternoon was agonising. I never had such pulling; all the time the sledge rasps and creaks.... We have covered 6 miles but at fearful cost to ourselves."

They reached the South Pole on January 18, 1912 and found Amundsen's tent and note. Weakened and disheartened, they faced the return journey. All of them died on the way back.

KEY DATES IN ANTARCTIC EXPLORATION

1820	First sighting claimed by Russian, British, and American expeditions
1837–40	Adélie Land discovered and claimed for France by Dumont d'Urville
1838–42	American Charles Wilkes explores East Antarctic coast
1839–43	James Clark Ross discovers Ross Sea and explores Victoria Land
1898	Belgian ship *Belgica* becomes trapped in ice, forcing crew to be the first people to spend a winter in Antarctica
1899	First planned over-wintering onshore by British Southern Cross Expedition led by Carsten Egeberg Borchgrevink
1901–13	Robert Falcon Scott and Ernest Shackleton pioneer routes into the interior as part of scientific investigations
1909	South Magnetic Pole discovered by Douglas Mawson
1911	South Pole reached by Roald Amundsen
1928	First airplane landing in Antarctica
1957–58	First crossing of Antarctica by the Commonwealth Trans-Antarctic Expedition

EXPLORING FARTHER AFIELD

After Scott and Amundsen, other explorers led expeditions to other parts of Antarctica, much of which was still completely unknown. In 1914 Ernest Shackleton embarked on the Imperial Trans-Antarctic Expedition. The following winter, his ship, *Endurance,* became trapped and crushed by pack ice in the Weddell Sea. Shackleton set out alone in an open boat on an 800-mile journey from Elephant Island, near the tip of the Antarctic Peninsula, to South Georgia. There he summoned help and returned with a party of rescuers to save his crew.

The next large-scale explorations began in 1928, with expeditions from Australia and the United States. The Australian Hubert Wilkins made the first airplane flights over the continent and surveyed the Antarctic Peninsula, and the American Richard Byrd also used aircraft to explore east of the Ross Ice Shelf. Byrd led three more expeditions in the 1930s and 1940s.

INTERNATIONAL GEOPHYSICAL YEAR (IGY)

International Geophysical Year was an international scientific project, involving 67 nations, to explore the earth and the space around it. It lasted from July 1957 to December 1958, although the planning for it began several years earlier. One of the special programs was Antarctic research, because half the continent had still not been seen by humans.

Research stations in Antarctica. This map shows those that are occupied all year round. There are about 25 other summer-only bases and dozens of abandoned stations.

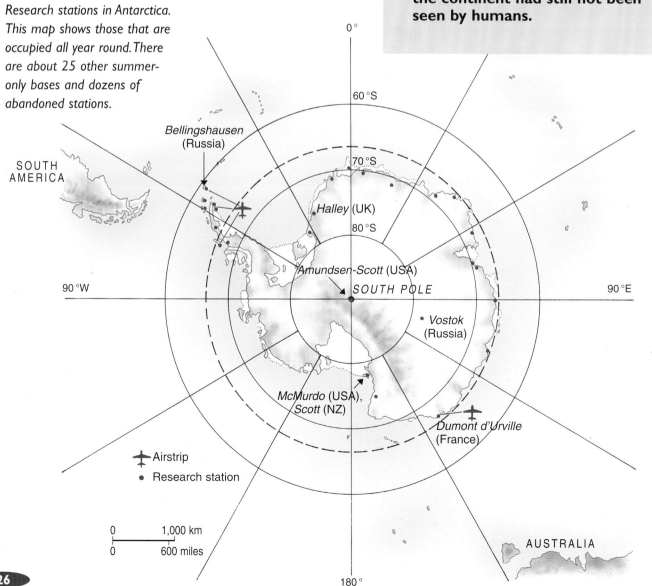

0°

60°S

Bellingshausen (Russia)

SOUTH AMERICA

70°S

Halley (UK)

80°S

Amundsen-Scott (USA)

90°W

90°E

SOUTH POLE

Vostok (Russia)

McMurdo (USA), Scott (NZ)

Dumont d'Urville (France)

Airstrip

Research station

0   1,000 km

0   600 miles

AUSTRALIA

180°

International interest in Antarctica grew after the end of World War II in 1945, and the foundations for today's extensive scientific research programs were laid in the 1950s, especially during International Geophysical Year, 1957–8 (see box). The highlight of Antarctic research during International Geophysical Year was the crossing of the continent by Vivian Fuchs's Commonwealth Trans-Antarctic Expedition in 1957–8. In addition, 50 research stations were established in Antarctica at which scientists from 12 nations could live and work during the winter as well as the summer. Supplies were brought to these stations by ship, air, and motorized sleds. The year was extremely successful. It revolutionized understanding not only of the region, but of the rest of the world as well. It also led to the Antarctic Treaty in 1959, which created a peaceful future for Antarctica.

Above *Vivian Fuchs, who led the successful Commonwealth Trans-Antarctic Expedition, with other members of his team. (Vivian Fuchs has a pipe in his mouth.)*

Right *An American research station at McMurdo Sound, Ross Island. The United States was the first country to make intercontinental flights to Antarctica.*

TERRITORIAL CLAIMS

Much of history is the story of people or nations trying to acquire more land and resources for themselves. For example, the Americas were first settled by people who came from Asia, but they were displaced by migrants from Europe who claimed the land for European countries such as Spain, Portugal, Great Britain, and France. European countries divided the whole of Africa among themselves without any consideration for the local people who lived there.

One of the reasons for national scientific and exploration expeditions to Antarctica was to support territorial claims. In other words, the countries wanted to take parts of Antarctica and own them so that they would be able to use any resources that might be discovered there. It is known, for example, that there is coal on the continent and oil under the ocean bed.

Many countries have been involved in the discovery, exploration, and scientific investigation of Antarctica. Seven of them have made territorial claims, sometimes for the same piece of land. For example, Great Britain, Chile, and Argentina all have claims on the peninsula stretching toward South America. Such competing claims led to each country using its own set of place names, to the confusion of the rest of the world. At least, they have managed to agree on a new name for the area until the claims are resolved—the Antarctic Peninsula. Other countries have refused to recognize any of these territorial claims.

Almost all of Antarctica is claimed by at least one country, and some parts are claimed by two or even three nations. The distribution of research stations (see the map on page 26) is related to these territorial claims. In the past, the USSR built stations in each of the sectors claimed by other nations, while the United States put a station at the South Pole to cover all the claimed sectors. Great Britain, Chile, Argentina, and Australia all built several bases in the sectors they claimed. Some of the bases still seem to exist more to back up sovereignty claims than for any scientific purpose.

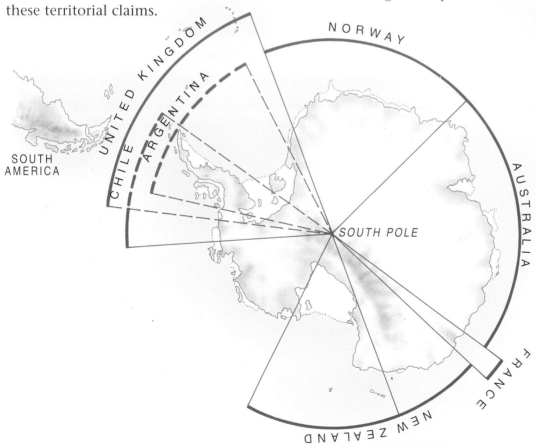

THE ANTARCTIC TREATY 1959

The International Geophysical Year (see pages 26 and 27) was very important for scientific research in Antarctica. Many nations worked together to find out more about the region and what influence it had on the rest of the world. It was so successful that a decision was made to try and maintain the cooperation. In 1959 the Antarctic Treaty was agreed by the 12 nations that had set up bases in Antarctica during IGY, and it came into operation in 1961.

The treaty is still in force and is working very well. It has enabled scientists from around the world to work together. Even Russian and Western scientists were able to work together during the cold war, when relations between East and West were very strained. The knowledge gained from the research has been invaluable to all countries. For example, without it we may never have learned that there was a problem with the ozone layer.

The flags of 12 nations fly at the South Pole. Behind is the dome of the American Amundsen-Scott base. The dome is 55 ft. high and houses everything scientists need to live and work there.

TREATY TERMS

The Antarctic Treaty covers all land and ice shelves south of latitude 60° South, but not the oceans, which are covered by separate treaties. There are 14 parts to the treaty, but the main points are

- No military use will be made of Antarctica
- Countries are able to carry out any scientific programs they want
- Countries will share scientific information
- The territorial claims will remain, but not be discussed further
- There will be no nuclear explosions and no disposal of nuclear waste
- The treaty can be reviewed and amended after 30 years

ANTARCTICA'S NATURAL RESOURCES

Scientists are trying to find out as much as possible about Antarctica and its surrounding seas. Part of this research includes finding out what resources are found in the region.

MINERALS

Oil and natural gas are thought to exist in the continental shelf that extends under the sea around Antarctica. There are also claims that the continent is as rich in minerals as Southern Africa and South America, to which it was once attached. However, 40 years of geological mapping have not uncovered much evidence of this.

Some iron ore has been found in eastern Antarctica, and there are coal seams running through the Transantarctic Mountains, but the quantities are not thought to be worth mining, especially in such inhospitable conditions. Prospecting for minerals like oil would normally be done by private companies, but as there is a ban on mining on the continent until at least 2041, there is little incentive to go prospecting.

Below A scientist stands next to an exposed coal seam in the Glossopteris Valley in the Transantarctic Mountains.

RESOURCES OF THE OCEAN

The major natural resources of the Antarctic Ocean are whales, seals, and fish. Seal hunters were among the first explorers of the region. They came especially to hunt fur seals, whose fur was used to make hats and felt. By the 1920s, hunters had slaughtered so many that probably fewer than 100 remained alive—too few to bother hunting.

Other types of seals were also hunted. The southern elephant seal is the largest Antarctic seal, growing to almost 22 ft. in length. It was hunted for its blubber, which was boiled down to make a very high-quality oil. Almost 265 gallons could be obtained from one large elephant seal. There was a thriving industry on South Georgia, processing the carcasses of whales and seals brought in by the hunters' boats.

The fur and elephant seals were hunted almost to extinction. Today, all seal hunting is controlled by international treaty, and the numbers have recovered. There is no commercial hunting of seals, and it seems they will never be hunted again on such a scale.

Above Elephant seals are the largest of the six species of seals that live in Antarctica. A male can weigh up to 4 tons and measure 22 feet in length. Elephant seals spend most of their lives at sea, only coming ashore to breed.

FLOATING FISH FACTORIES

Antarctica's fish resources are plentiful, partly because the whales that used to eat them have been hunted and killed. Fishing vessels are able to fish in this remote region because catches can be taken to large factory ships, where the fish is processed and frozen at sea. When they are full, the factory ships return to port to sell their cargo. Fish, squid, and 400,000 tons of krill a year are harvested from the waters surrounding Antarctica.

PROBLEMS OF EXPLOITING NATURAL RESOURCES

The population of the earth is almost six billion, and each person is a consumer of the earth's natural resources. The demand for resources is so great that few parts of the earth escape the interest of developers. Forests are cleared for their timber, for new agricultural land, golf courses, housing, and other land uses. Farmland is sold for the minerals below to be mined or for building new factories, shopping malls, roads, and housing projects. Arctic lands are mined for oil and valuable metals. The oceans are fished to supply us with food and fertilizers. Yet in Antarctica there is no economic development and very little pressure from business and industry even to explore the area to see what resources it might provide in the future. Why, when resources are in such demand, is there apparently so little interest in the commercial potential of Antarctica?

RRS Bransfield *makes its way through thick sea ice in the Weddell Sea. It is carrying supplies for the British Research Station, Halley.*

ISOLATION

When one looks at the earth from above the South Pole, apart from Antarctica there is very little land to be seen. The continent is isolated from the main centers of population and wealth, which are mostly in the Northern Hemisphere. This is where the main demand for resources lies and where most major industries are located. Distance alone discourages development on the Antarctic continent.

HARSH CONDITIONS

If oil, gas, and minerals are mined in the Arctic region, why could they not be mined in Antarctica? It is because, compared with Antarctica, the conditions in the Arctic are quite mild. Antarctica is so much colder that working outside for any length of time is impossible. The almost constant winds increase the problems. In addition, the covering of ice—which is always moving—makes the mining of any minerals below it a huge and expensive technical problem. The cost of overcoming the problems would be so great that mining companies could not make a profit.

Anyone developing Antarctica would also have to pay for everything the industry and the workers needed. There are no roads, power supplies, waste disposal facilities, houses, stores, or other facilities that people usually take for granted. Working in Antarctica would probably not attract many people, so wages would have to be very high.

THE PROBLEM OF SOVEREIGNTY

There is no agreement on which countries rule Antarctica, so commercial companies would have to negotiate with all the countries that have signed the Antarctic Treaty before being able to work there. The huge cost involved in developing any resources in Antarctica has made it easier for countries to make agreements that limit development and protect the environment. The Protocol on Environmental Protection (1991) includes a 50-year ban on mining.

Blizzard conditions, like these on the Ross Ice Shelf, make walking difficult.

WHALING

While the continent of Antarctica itself has remained relatively free of development, the resources of the surrounding ocean have been plundered. Whales have been hunted in the oceans of the world for centuries, as a cheap source of oil, whalebone, meat, and other products. Wherever commercial whaling has taken place, a similar story has unfolded. When the hunters discovered a new hunting ground, they killed as many whales as possible, often wiping out the species that were most valuable to them. The hunters then moved farther afield to do the same in another area.

That is how whale hunters came to Antarctica. By the end of the 19th century there were too few whales left elsewhere for the American, Dutch, English, Japanese, Norwegian, Russian, and Spanish hunters. The profits from whaling were so high that the hunters could afford to catch whales even in such a remote and difficult environment. Some technological advances, such as harpoon guns, steamships, and factory ships, also made hunting easier.

Above A disused whaling station at Leith Harbor, South Georgia. In the 19th and early 20th centuries, whales caught in Antarctic waters were taken to stations like this for processing.

Below Whalers found a profitable use for most of their catch and very little was wasted.

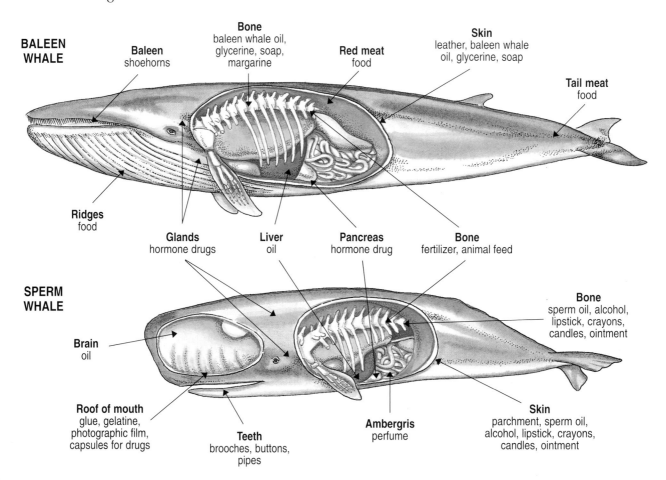

BALEEN WHALE

Baleen shoehorns

Bone baleen whale oil, glycerine, soap, margarine

Red meat food

Skin leather, baleen whale oil, glycerine, soap

Tail meat food

Ridges food

Glands hormone drugs

Liver oil

Pancreas hormone drug

Bone fertilizer, animal feed

SPERM WHALE

Brain oil

Roof of mouth glue, gelatine, photographic film, capsules for drugs

Teeth brooches, buttons, pipes

Ambergris perfume

Bone sperm oil, alcohol, lipstick, crayons, candles, ointment

Skin parchment, sperm oil, alcohol, lipstick, crayons, candles, ointment

Since the 1920s more than 1.3 million whales have been killed in the waters around Antarctica. The number of large whales was reduced to a tiny fraction of what it used to be, and some species were on the verge of extinction by the middle of the 20th century. In 1949 the International Whaling Commission (IWC) was set up to regulate the whaling industry, but it was totally ineffective. As public pressure to "Save the Whale" built up in the 1970s, and more scientific evidence of the seriousness of the situation became available, a halt on commercial whaling was finally approved. Japan continued catching some species of whale for what were called scientific purposes. However, there were so few of the larger whales left by that time that most of the traditional whaling countries had already given up whaling because it was not economical. In 1994, the IWC declared a Southern Ocean Sanctuary, which protects whales from commercial hunting south of 40° S.

Above *A Japanese whaling ship in the Ross Sea with a catch of minke whales. The minke is the only baleen whale that can be caught legally in Antarctic waters.*

A MORAL ISSUE?

In recent years, the stocks of some whales have increased and some countries of the IWC consider that hunting these types could begin again as long as it is carefully controlled. However, there is still a lot of opposition to whaling. It has now become a moral issue. Whales are probably the next most intelligent creatures after humans. Like us, they communicate with one another, have evolved social structures, and appear to have feelings. To hunt and kill such beings, especially in such a cruel way, is considered wrong by many people.

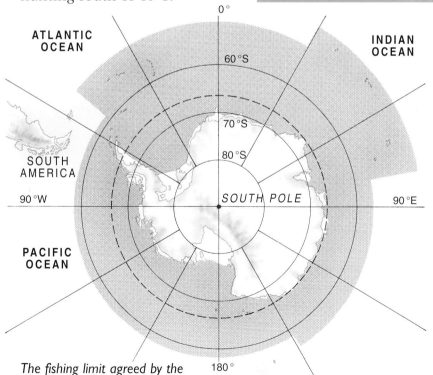

The fishing limit agreed by the Convention on the Conservation of Antarctic Marine Living Resources (CCAMLR) in 1982. It is intended to ensure that enough fish are left for penguins, seals, and whales to eat.

FISHING

The ocean around Antarctica was also rich in fish, and this attracted fishing fleets to the area. For some types of fish, it took only a few years to reduce the stock to less than five percent of what it was before. As one species became scarce, the fleets turned their attention to another.

To keep a serious situation from becoming disastrous, in 1982 the Antarctic Treaty countries agreed the Convention on the Conservation of Antarctic Marine Living Resources. It attempts to protect the ecosystem of the ocean as a whole, rather than individual species within that ecosystem. It uses scientific research to make laws that try to prevent damage before it happens. However, marine scientists do not believe it is working very well.

SCIENTIFIC RESEARCH

The Antarctic Treaty of 1959 established Antarctica as a continent for international cooperation in scientific, nonmilitary research. Since then, Antarctica has become a laboratory for finding out about the evolution of the earth and how it is changing today, often as a result of human activities.

The starting point for research is to obtain basic information about Antarctica—its shape, size, relief, climate, ecology, ice movements, and the ways in which they affect one another. Some of these are measured constantly so that any long-term changes can be detected. Scientists have shown that what happens elsewhere on the earth has an effect on Antarctica and that Antarctica also influences what happens over the rest of the earth.

ICE CORES AND CLIMATE

The ice sheet over Antarctica has accumulated over thousands of years. Each year fresh snow falls on the surface, compressing the layers below into ice that has remained undisturbed. By drilling down into the ice and removing a core, scientists can tell how old the ice is. By analyzing the air and particles of dust or pollen in the ice, it is possible to discover what the earth's climatic conditions were like at the time. Ice cores more than 160,000 years old have been brought to the surface. Analysis of them shows that the climate in Antarctica has fluctuated considerably in the past. Ice from the last 100 years shows an increasing amount of air pollution, mainly as a result of industrialization in Europe and North America.

Right *Scientists take ice cores on the polar plateau near the South Pole.*

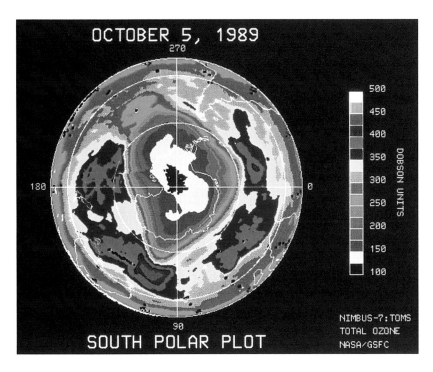

OCTOBER 5, 1989
270
500
450
400
350
300
250
200
150
100
DOBSON UNITS
180
0
90
SOUTH POLAR PLOT
NIMBUS-7:TOMS
TOTAL OZONE
NASA/GSFC

Above *This picture, taken by the Nimbus 7 satellite, shows clearly how the ozone layer has become thinner over Antarctica. The purple shades mark the areas where the ozone layer is thinnest.*

OZONE OVER ANTARCTICA

Ozone is a gas found in small amounts in the stratosphere, one of the layers that makes up the earth's atmosphere. Without it the sun's ultraviolet light can reach the surface. Ultraviolet light can harm all living things. In humans, it can affect our eyesight, cause skin cancer, and damage DNA, the molecules that carry the information that makes us what we are.

In 1977, a researcher with the British Antarctic Survey discovered that the amount of ozone in the atmosphere 7.5 to 13 mi. above the continent decreased dramatically in the Antarctic spring. Little attention was paid to the discovery since people thought the instruments must be faulty. But then in 1987 the Nimbus 7 satellite, which was programmed to measure ozone, found a similar reduction.

Following this discovery, measurements have been made in other parts of the earth. A thinning of the ozone layer over the Arctic was found. This was considered very serious because many people live in northern latitudes and there is much agriculture. Warnings are now given when the ozone layer is reduced so that people can cover their skin.

The main causes of the problem are CFCs—chemicals that are used in refrigerators, air conditioners, the electronics industry, and aerosols—and halons used in firefighting equipment. The leaders of many countries agreed to begin phasing out CFCs and halons, but the chemicals take so long to break down in the atmosphere that it will take at least another 50 years before the ozone layer recovers.

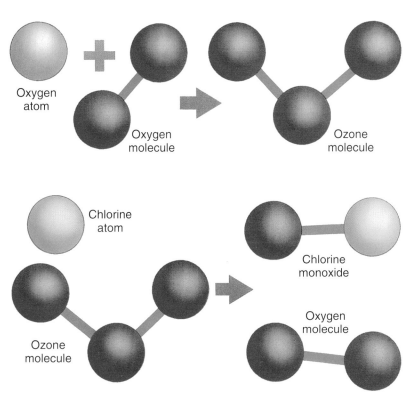

Oxygen atom

Oxygen molecule

Ozone molecule

Chlorine atom

Ozone molecule

Chlorine monoxide

Oxygen molecule

Left *When an oxygen molecule and a free oxygen atom combine, an ozone molecule is formed. The sun's ultraviolet radiation breaks up CFCs in the atmosphere, releasing free chlorine atoms. When a free chlorine atom collides with an ozone molecule in the earth's ozone layer, it takes one of its oxygen atoms, destroying the ozone molecule.*

CONSERVATION AND DEVELOPMENT

Antarctica is the only continent that has remained free of all commercial development. Only scientific research is allowed. There are many people and some countries that would like this situation to remain forever by making Antarctica into a world park. There are others who believe that it should be possible to develop the resources of Antarctica as elsewhere in the world. They accept that any development would have to be controlled so that there would be no serious damage to the environment.

THE PROS AND CONS OF DEVELOPMENT

AGAINST

Antarctica is the last great wilderness and should remain so.

Research programs require the environment to remain as near natural as possible.

Not enough is known about the Antarctic environment to know how it might be affected by development. It takes the environment a long time to recover from any damage in such a cold climate.

The resources will only last a few decades. It would be better to invest money in finding ways to reduce our use of resources.

FOR

Developers have experience of how to protect the environment in the Arctic.

Strict control can be imposed on developers to minimize any environmental change.

Allowing some development would provide an opportunity to find out the effect of development on the environment.

The world's population is increasing, and people require new resources to support them.

Right When oil was discovered at Prudhoe Bay in Alaska, inside the Arctic Circle, this refinery was built to process the oil, and tanks were constructed to store it. If oil were to be extracted in Antarctica, similar facilities might be needed there.

THE BATTLE FOR ANTARCTICA

The Antarctic Treaty of 1959 helped keep the continent free of all commercial development for 30 years. At the end of that period, countries could ask for changes to the treaty, but any changes would have to be agreed by all the other countries. In 1989 a group of countries had prepared a set of proposals that, if accepted, would have allowed mineral resources to be developed. The set of proposals was called the Convention for the Regulation of Antarctic Mineral Resource Activities, usually referred to as CRAMRA. They were strongly opposed by a few countries and by most environmentalists. The stage was set for a battle between the protectionists and the developers, and the outcome would determine the future of Antarctica after 1989.

France and Australia refused to sign the new convention and said that Antarctica should become a world park where protection of the environment is most important. This idea was turned down by other countries and a compromise was suggested. Discussions continued for two years, when it looked like a revision to the treaty had been agreed by everyone and could at last be signed. The revision banned all mining for 50 years. However, at the last minute, the United States refused to sign. It did not like the clause that said at the end of the 50-year period the ban could only be overturned if all the treaty nations agreed. After much pressure from other nations, the United States finally relented, but only after concessions had been made.

The new agreement, called the Protocol on Environmental Protection, is an addition to the original treaty. All mining and mineral extraction is banned until 2041, after which the ban can be lifted if 75 percent of the members of the Antarctic Treaty agree. For the time being, the continent has been spared from the risks of development.

Above *These scientists from New Zealand have set up camp away from their base to carry out research in the Transantarctic Mountains.*

Above *Garbage left behind when research bases are abandoned spoils the Antarctic landscape. Rusting debris can also harm wildlife and cause pollution.*

THE HUMAN IMPACT

Even without commercial development, the Antarctic environment has been damaged by explorers and scientists. Scientists need shelter, laboratories, regular deliveries of supplies, and transportation to scientific sites and other bases, and they produce considerable quantities of waste. Scientific bases have accumulated garbage, and they have burned or disposed of it in the sea. The sites were often untidy, with leaking fuel drums and waste contaminating the land. Old bases were just abandoned with no attempt to restore the environment.

In 1983, France began building a long runway at Dumont d'Urville so that it could use large Hercules transport planes to supply its scientists. There was much opposition from environmentalists, and a survey was done to assess how much damage the runway would cause. The survey team recommended that it should be abandoned because of the environmental damage it would cause, but in 1987 building continued anyway. Five islands inhabited by emperor penguins were blown up to provide the materials for its construction.

Left *The French airstrip at Dumont d'Urville in January 1995*

In 1989 an Argentinian supply ship sank off the Western Antarctic Peninsula, spilling more than a million gallons of diesel fuel into the sea. It affected bird and marine life in the area. The environmental damage of such accidents is likely to be long lasting, because diesel fuel takes 100 times longer to break down in Antarctica than in a warmer climate.

GREENPEACE IN ANTARCTICA

In 1983, Greenpeace began a campaign to protect Antarctica. To find out what was really happening there, it set up the Greenpeace Antarctic Expedition. From 1986 the group visited the region to find out for itself how well the environment was being respected. It also decided to try and set a good example to the others and established a base in 1987. The organization demonstrated successfully that it is possible to work in Antarctica without causing damage to the environment. When Greenpeace left in 1992, the base was dismantled and removed completely.

Below *Each year a small number of tourists travel to Antarctica to see sights such as these king penguins at St. Andrews Bay, South Georgia.*

ANTARCTIC TOURISM

Not all commercial exploitation of Antarctica is banned. A few tourists visit the continent in summer, mainly to see the wildlife. Visiting Antarctica has its dangers: In 1979, 257 people were killed when an airplane carrying sightseers from New Zealand crashed into Mount Erebus.

Some industries produce large amounts of greenhouse gases, which add to global warming. If the earth continues to get warmer, the Antarctic ice could begin to melt rapidly.

ANTARCTICA AND THE GLOBAL ENVIRONMENT

Antarctica has a unique environment because of its position and isolation. However, its protection depends on more than controlling what happens on and around Antarctica. Its environment is affected by environmental changes elsewhere in the world. In turn, changes in Antarctica affect the environments of the rest of the world.

THE OZONE LAYER

The thinning of the ozone layer over Antarctica has been known about since 1977. Since then it has grown worse, and although there is now an agreement that countries will stop using chemicals that affect the ozone layer, it will be some time before improvements are noticed. Meanwhile, damaging ultraviolet radiation will continue to affect Antarctica. Research has shown that the food supply for fish, whales, birds, and seals declines when radiation levels are high.

CHANGING CLIMATE

Burning fossil fuels, such as coal, gas, and oil, raises the amount of carbon dioxide in the earth's atmosphere. Carbon dioxide is called a greenhouse gas because it absorbs heat that would otherwise escape into space. Most scientists now agree that the extra carbon dioxide accumulating in the atmosphere is causing the earth to warm up. The warming effect seems to be greatest in the polar regions. The average temperature of the Antarctic Peninsula has risen by 4.5° F since the 1940s, an increase about ten times as fast as the global average over the last century.

As the temperature has risen, the amount of ice covering the ocean near Antarctica has decreased. Ice is very important in controlling temperature because it does not absorb the sun's heat but reflects it back into space. If the area covered by ice decreases, more heat is absorbed by the sea. This makes temperatures still higher, so more ice melts, and so on.

Antarctica contains about 90 percent of the world's ice. The ice is diminishing at the rate of half a million tons a year, adding to the amount of water in the sea and causing the sea level to rise. This threatens coastal communities around the world with frequent flooding and eventual loss of their land. If the Antarctic ice sheet were to melt completely, the sea level would rise by 215 ft., about the height of a 15-story building, but this is unlikely to happen in the foreseeable future.

Unusually warm weather in Antarctica has caused ice and snow to melt leaving this meltwater pool.

SHARED RESPONSIBILITY

The future of Antarctica's unique environment does not only depend on what people do in Antarctica, but also on what we all do. The main threats at the moment are the thinning of the ozone layer as a result of using chemicals like CFCs, and global warming, which is mainly caused by burning fossil fuels.

THE FUTURE

Much has been written about the future of Antarctica. During the 1960s there was a belief that with modern technology anything could be achieved. There were visions of permanent settlements built under huge transparent domes, supplied with energy from nuclear power stations. Other ideas included creating settlements within the ice itself. Such scenes are only likely to become reality if huge deposits of natural resources are found and it is agreed they can be extracted.

STRATEGY FOR A SUSTAINABLE FUTURE

There is agreement that the main activity in Antarctica should be scientific research and that the environment should be protected. The research programs in Antarctica are valuable to us all. They help scientists learn more about how the earth's natural systems work and how human activities around the world are affecting them. With this information, global problems can be identified and action taken to resolve them before it is too late. The international agreements to phase out CFCs and other chemicals that damage the ozone layer are a direct result of research that began in Antarctica.

Antarctica is also a particularly good place from which to study the upper atmosphere. This is the zone in which navigation and communication satellites orbit. Magnetic storms can disrupt their operation, causing problems for people on the ground. Trying to forecast when such storms will occur is as important as weather forecasting is on the ground.

Research in Antarctica is expensive, so it makes good sense for countries to work together on projects, to avoid doing similar research and to share their results. The international Scientific Committee on Antarctic Research (SCAR) has done a lot to help such cooperation.

In the future, national research programs and bases may be replaced by an international program carried out from a few international bases. Each of the bases will be environmentally friendly, making use of wind and solar energy and producing very little waste. When they are no longer needed, the bases will be dismantled and removed, leaving little trace that humans were ever there.

THREATS TO ANTARCTICA

Antarctica's environment is relatively safe for the time being. However, should valuable resources such as oil and gas be found, pressure to allow mining will increase as these resources become scarce elsewhere in the world. However carefully controlled, development will mean the end of the earth's last unspoiled wilderness. We can all help to prevent this by not wasting resources.

Below A plastic ozone research balloon is about to be released by American scientists at McMurdo Station on Ross Island. To many scientists, Antarctica is a valuable laboratory in which to study the earth and its atmosphere.

Opposite Adélie penguins leaping into the icy waters around Antarctica. Adélies are one of several species of penguin that are perfectly adapted to the freezing Antarctic conditions.

ANTARCTICA WORLD PARK

Some people favor the idea of Antarctica becoming a world park, where the priorities of environmental protection and scientific research guide people's activities. In the Antarctic World Park mining, military, and nuclear activities, the disposal of radioactive and other dangerous wastes, and interference with plants, sea mammals, and birds would all be prohibited. Activities allowed would include scientific research, setting up and supplying research bases, some tourism, and fishing.

GLOSSARY

Axis The earth's axis is an imaginary line drawn between the North and South poles, around which the earth rotates.

Colonize When people or animals settle or establish themselves in a new environment.

Commercial/economic development When people, businesses, or countries use the earth's resources for profit.

Continental drift The slow movement of the continents over the surface of the earth.

Continental shelf The seabed surrounding a continent at depths of up to about 650 feet. Beyond the continental shelf, the seabed slopes steeply to the ocean floor.

Ecosystem A group of plants and animals and the physical environment in which they live.

Extinction When a species of animals or plants dies out completely.

Frostbite Damage to parts of the body that do not get enough blood when exposed to extreme cold.

Glacier A mass of ice moving slowly downhill along a valley.

Geologists Scientists who study the origin, history, and structure of the earth.

Hemisphere Half of the earth.

Lichen A plant formed by the combination of an alga and a fungus, usually found on bare rock. The alga produces food for the fungus, and the fungus retains moisture that the alga needs to survive.

Latitude How far north or south of the equator something is. Lines of latitude are imaginary lines that circle the earth in an east-west direction.

Longitude How far east or west of the Greenwich Meridian something is. Lines of longitude are imaginary lines that circle the earth in a north-south direction, passing through the North and South poles.

Mammals Animals that are warm blooded, breathe air, and suckle their young—for example, humans, whales, and seals.

Migrate To travel between different habitats during certain seasons of the year.

Mirage An optical illusion—usually the image of a distant object or a sheet of water—caused by light rays being distorted as they pass through the atmosphere close to the ground. Mirages can occur in very cold places and in very hot deserts.

Natural resources Materials, such as iron and wood, that are used by humans but provided by nature.

Nutrients Substances in food that provide nourishment needed to help keep a plant or animal alive.

Orbit The curved path followed by a satellite, planet, or comet around another body.

Ozone layer A layer of ozone gas in the earth's atmosphere that shields us from some of the sun's harmful ultraviolet rays.

Pack ice The ice that forms when the sea freezes over large areas.

Peninsula A narrow strip of land jutting out into the sea from the mainland.

Plankton Microscopic plants and animals that drift in the sea or lakes.

Precipitation All forms of moisture deposited on the earth's surface, including rain and snow.

Predator An animal that preys on other animals for its food.

Protocol A formal international agreement.

Seismic research The use of sound waves to analyze geological structures beneath the surface.

Snow blindness Temporary and very painful blindness caused by the reflection of sunlight from a bright surface such as snow or ice.

Species Animals and plants that look similar to each other and can breed to produce similar offspring.

Subtropical The characteristics of the regions bordering on the tropics.

Scurvy A disease, caused by the lack of vitamin C, that killed many early explorers.

Treaty A formal agreement, usually made between two or more countries.

Ultraviolet Rays of light from the sun that cannot be seen by the human eye and can cause damage to living cells.

FURTHER INFORMATION

Organizations to contact

Greenpeace
1436 U Street NW
Washington, DC 20003

National Wildlife Federation
1412 16th Street, NW
Washington, DC 20036

Books to read

Billings, Henry. *Antarctica*. Enchantment of the World. Danbury, CT: Children's Press, 1994.

Flaherty, Leo and Goetzmann, William H. *Roald Amundsen & The Quest for the South Pole*. World Explorers. New York: Chelsea House, 1993.

George, Michael. *Antarctica*. Mankato, MN: Creative Education, Inc., 1994.

Hackwell, John W. *Desert of Ice: Life and Work in Antarctica*. Old Tappan, NJ: Simon and Schuster Childrens, 1991.

McMillan, Bruce. *Summer Ice, Antarctic Life*. Boston: Houghton Mifflin, 1995.

Poncet, Sally. *South Georgia*. Old Tappan, NJ: Simon and Schuster Childrens, 1995.

Sauvain, Phillip. *Robert Scott in the Antarctic*. Great Twentieth Century Expeditions. Morristown, NJ: Silver Burdett Press, 1993.

Stewart, Gail B. *Antarctica*. Places in the News. Morristown, NJ: Silver Burdett Press, 1991.

Winckler, Suzanne and Rodgers, Mary M. *Our Endangered Planet: Antarctica*. Minneapolis, MN: Lerner Group, 1991.

Woods, Michael. *Science on Ice: Research in the Antarctic*. Brookfield, CT: Millbrook Press, 1995.

INDEX

The figures in **bold** refer to photographs

Adélie land 25
Adélie penguins **45**
Amoux's beaked whale 20
Amundsen, Roald 22, **24**, 24, 25, 26
Angaraland 8
Antarctic Circle **6**, 7
Antarctic Convergence **16**, 16
Antarctic Peninsula **4**, 7, 9, **10**, 10, 12, 13, 26, 28, 41, 43
Arctic 6, 15, 18, 24, 32, 33, 37, 38
Arctic Circle **6**, 38
Arctic tern 21
Argentina 28
Atlantic Ocean 7, 16
atmosphere **12**, 12, 37, 43, 44
Australia 6, 18, 26, 28, 39

baleen whales 19, 20, **34**
Belgica 25
birds 21, 41, 42, 45
blizzards 12, 23, **33**
blue whale **20**, 20
Borchgrevink, Carsten Egeberg 25
British Southern Cross Expedition 23, 25
Bryde's whale **20**
Byrd, Richard 26

Cape Horn 16
carbon dioxide 43
CFCs **37**, 37, 43, 44
Chile 28
claims, territorial **28**, 28, 29, 30
climate 8, 12, 13, 21, 36, 38, 41, 43
clothing 12, **13**, 13
coal 6, 8, 28, **30**, 30, 43
Colobanthus 18
Commonwealth Trans-Antarctic Expedition 25, **27**, 27
continental drift **8**, 8
Convention for the Regulation of Antarctic Mineral Resource Activities (CRAMRA) 39
Convention on the Conservation of Antarctic Marine Living Resources (CCAMLR) **35**, 35
core samples **36**, 36

Dumont d'Urville, Jules-Sébastien-César 25, 40
development 32, 33, 34, 38, 39, 40, 44
dogs 24, 25
dolphins 19
dry valleys 10, **11**
dysentery 23

Elephant Island 26
elephant seals 19, **31**, 31
emperor penguins **6**, **21**, 21, 40
Endurance 26

fertilizers 32
fin whale **20**, 20
fishing 31, 35, 45
France 15, 25, 28, 39, 40
frostbite 13, 23
Fuchs, Vivian **27**, 27
fur seals 19, 31

Gamburtsev Mountains 9
Germany 23
glaciers 10, **14**, 17
global warming 42, 43
Gondwanaland 8
Great Britain 23, 28
greenhouse gases 42, 43
Greenpeace Antarctic Expedition 41

halons 37
humpback whale **20**, 20

icebergs **15**, 15, 17
icebreakers **17**, 17
Imperial Trans-Antarctic Expedition 26
International Geophysical Year (IGY) 26, 27, 29
International Whaling Commission (IWC) 35
iron ore 30

Japan 34, 35

killer whales 19, **20**, 20
king penguins 21, **41**
krill **19**, 19, 20, 31

Laurasia 8
leopard seals 19
lichens **18**, 18
long-finned pilot whale 20

McMurdo Sound 10, 11, 23, 24, 27
Mawson, Douglas 25
metals 32
midnight sun **6**, 7
minerals 6, 17, 30, 32, 33
mining 6, 30, 33, 39, 44, 45
minke whale **20**, 20, **35**
mirages 5
mosses **18**, 18
Mount Erebus 11, 41

New Zealand 41
Nimbus 7 satellite 37

ocean currents 12, **16**, 16, 17
oil 6, 28, 30, 32, 33, **38**, 43, 44
Olympus Range **11**
ozone 29, **37**, 37, 42, 43, 44

Pacific Ocean 7, 16
pack ice **7**, **15**, 15, **17**, 17, 22, 26, **32**
parhelions 5
penguins 6, 19, **21**, 21, 35, 40, **45**
phytoplankton **19**, 19
plants 6, 8, **18**, 18, 19
pollution 36, **40**, 40

porpoises 19
Portugal 28
Protocol on Environmental Protection 33, 39

Queen Maud Land 22

research bases 18, 24, 25, **26**, 26, **27**, 29, **40**, 40, 41, **44**
Ross Ice Shelf 24, 26, **33**
Ross Island **5**, **27**, **44**
Ross, James Clark 11, 22, 25
Ross Sea 7, 10, 11, 15, 22, 25, **35**

Scientific Committee on Antarctic Research (SCAR) 44
Scott, Robert Falcon 23, 24, **25**, 25, 26
seals **19**, 19, 23, **31**, 31, 35, 42
sei whale **20**, 20
seismic research **9**, 9
Shackleton, Ernest 12, **23**, 23, 24, 25, 26
snow blindness 13, 23
South Georgia 26, 31, **33**, **41**
South Magnetic Pole 23, 25
South Pole 4, 7, 8, 12, 23, **24**, 24, 25, **29**, 32, 36
southern Bottlenose whale 20
southern right whale 20
Spain 28
sperm whale 20, **34**
squid 19, 20, 21, 31
storms 16, 44
Sweden 23

temperatures 4, 5, 12, 13, 15, 16, 17, 18, 21, 23, 43
Terra Australis Incognita 22
toothed whales 20
tourists **41**, 41
Transantarctic Mountains 8, 10, **30**, 30, 39

United States 26, 27, 28, 39

Victoria Land **11**, 22, 25
Vinson Massif 10

Weddell, James 23
Weddell Sea **6**, 7, 10, 23, 26, **32**
Weddell seal **19**
whales **19**, **20**, 20, 22, 23, 34, **35**
whaling 22, 23, 34, **35**, 35
white-out 5
Wilkes Land 22
Wilkes, Charles 22, 25
Wilkins, Hubert 26
wind 5, **12**, 12, 15, 16, 17, 33

zooplankton **19**